Honeybee Rescue
A Backyard Drama

Honeybee Rescue

A Backyard Drama

Loree Griffin Burns

photography by **Ellen Harasimowicz**

ini **Charlesbridge**

This is Mr. Connery, and that is his ramshackle barn.

The window with no glass opens into a garage with a badly leaking roof. A few days ago, on the way to his vegetable garden, Mr. Connery noticed that the rickety old structure was *buzzing*.

He poked his head inside the window hole . . .

. . . and discovered that a colony
of honeybees had moved in!

Mr. Connery keeps honeybees in wooden hive boxes in his yard. They collect nectar, and in the process, pollinate his plants.

The moment Mr. Connery saw bees building a hive in the garage, he knew what had happened: one of his colonies had outgrown its home.

Usually Mr. Connery notices when a family
of bees is getting too big for its wooden hive.
In response he stacks an additional box on top,
giving the bees room to spread out.

Sometimes though, a colony grows so fast that Mr. Connery misses the signs of overcrowding. When that happens, the bees deal with the problem on their own. They swarm.

What Is Swarming?

When squeezed for space, a honeybee colony splits itself in two.

The first step is to raise a new queen bee.

While the new queen is developing, the old queen and some of the hive's residents leave. They settle nearby in a hanging blob of clustered bees called a swarm.

The swarm stays put while hundreds of individual bees scout nearby for a place to settle permanently. When a suitable home is found, the swarm moves in and begins to make wax comb.

Back in the old hive, the new queen emerges. She and the remaining bees now have plenty of room.

scout bees coming and going

old queen
in the middle of the
swarm somewhere

By the time Mr. Connery found the garage bees, they were already making comb. They were not a swarm anymore, but a settled colony. Unfortunately they'd chosen a tumbledown structure for their new home. With its holes and leaks, the garage would offer little protection from the coming winter.

Mr. Connery knew these bees needed to move. So he called Mr. Nelson.

Mr. Nelson is a beekeeper who specializes in removing hives from dangerous places. He has rescued bees from inside fireplaces; from church steeples; and from ceilings, floors, and walls of family homes.

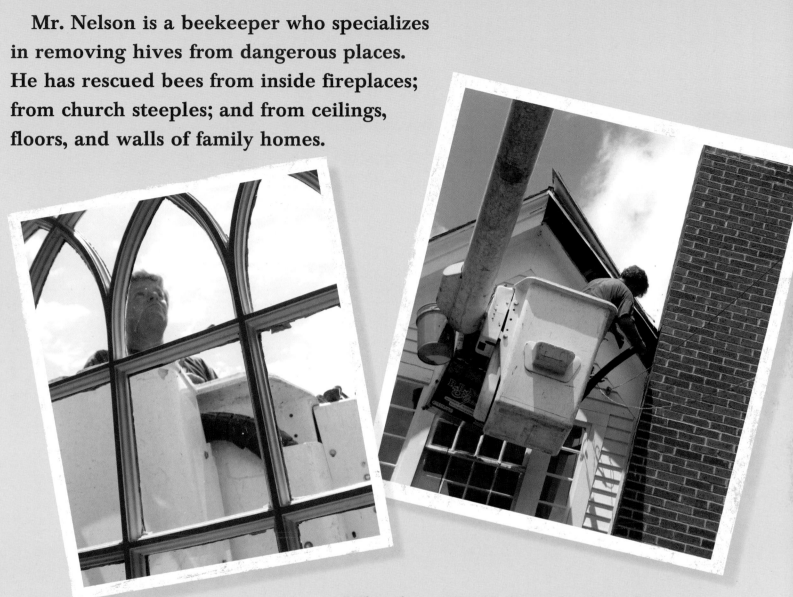

Why does Mr. Nelson do this? So the people who own those places don't exterminate vital pollinators. And because the unique structure of honeybee hives makes them surprisingly easy to relocate.

Hive Structure

The heart of a honeybee hive is its hanging sheets of golden comb. Bees produce wax flakes in their abdomens, then use their legs and mouths to mold the wax into long sheets of hexagon-shaped cups, or cells.

Bees use the cells to store pollen, nectar, and honey. They also raise young bees in them.

Wherever they make their home, honeybees prefer their sheets of comb to hang side by side, approximately one bee-body length apart.

comb inside tree

hive entrance

comb

wooden frame

comb inside
hive box

Together Mr. Nelson and Mr. Connery concoct a simple plan to move the garage bees back into a wooden hive box.

1. Clear the bees from the garage comb.

2. Cut the comb away from the ceiling.

3. Trim comb pieces to fit inside a new hive box.

But how will the two men start? How will they remove the thousands of honeybees crawling on and buzzing around the comb?

Believe it or not, a vacuum cleaner works nicely!
Not just any vacuum cleaner, mind you. Mr. Nelson
built one that is gentle. It's designed to keep tens of
thousands of sucked-up bees safe and out of the way
while he moves their home.

Honeybee Sucker-Upper

Mr. Nelson's bee-vac has two chambers that can be taken apart and lots of custom features to keep honeybees comfortable for the duration of their stay.

screened hole
to control suction strength

foam brush
to cushion incoming bees

bee-collection chamber
with room for 70,000 bees

lightweight wood
for easier carrying

large-diameter hose
to make the journey gentle

motor chamber

screen cover
to keep bees in the chamber and
allow air and water to reach them

Vacuuming bees requires both patience and stamina.

Standing on a ladder, Mr. Nelson drags the vacuum hose gently over the outside of the first sheet of comb. When it's clear of bees, he switches off his vacuum and sets down the hose.

Slowly so he doesn't further upset the bees, he uses a knife to cut the first sheet right across the middle. He carries the comb down to the garage floor.

He lays the bee-free side of the cut sheet against his bare arm, picks up the vacuum hose, and sucks up the bees on the other side. When he's done, Mr. Nelson gives the now-bee-free comb to Mr. Connery. Then he goes back up the ladder and repeats the entire process with the next piece.

Mr. Connery's job is to cut the comb into rectangles that will fit into the wooden frames of a hive box. He uses a metal gadget that Mr. Nelson designed and built. It looks like a giant cookie cutter.

For hours, Mr. Nelson vacuums bees and detaches sheets of comb.

For hours, Mr. Connery cuts the comb and fits it into hive frames.

Eventually about thirty-five thousand bees are crawling around in the collection chamber of Mr. Nelson's vacuum. Their trimmed comb is hanging in Mr. Connery's hive boxes.

Now it's time to reunite the two.

Mr. Nelson pours the garage bees from his vacuum into an empty hive box on a table. Mr. Connery quickly stacks the two boxes of garage-bee comb on top.

The two men set the new hive underneath the spot on the ceiling where the bees were living. Garage bees that are out collecting nectar and pollen on this perfect summer day will return to find their hive not *exactly* where they left it, but close enough.

They'll accept it.

Over the next two weeks, Mr. Connery will move the new hive a few feet every day. Eventually the bees will be back where they started, next to the garden and near the hive they swarmed out of a few months ago.

For today, though, there is only
one small task left: savoring some
garage-bee honey.

An Interview with Mr. Jon Nelson, bee rescuer

How did you get started in the bee-rescue business?

I rescued my first honeybee colony when I was twelve! My friends and I found a swarm, and we poked at it when we shouldn't have. My friend Tony got stung, and his mother wanted to kill the entire swarm. I ran home, looked up beekeepers in the phone book, and called one. He came and was soon scooping up bees *with his bare hands*, dumping them into a box he'd brought. "Aren't they going to sting you?" I asked him. "Not if I'm gentle," he said. "If you don't squeeze them, they won't sting you." I put on a bee veil to protect my face, and he let me dig my bare hands into the pile of bees, too. I didn't get a single sting.

And you've kept bees ever since?

I worked with bees on and off after that. What got me heavily into beekeeping more recently was colony collapse disorder (CCD). I have fruit trees and a garden on my property, but when CCD hit, I stopped seeing bees. I decided to become a full-time beekeeper.

How long does it take to rescue a colony of bees from a building or other structure?

We actually take a lot of time for the removal: four to eight hours. And then, sometimes, another two, three, or four hours at my house to put the hives all back together. It's a lot of work that not many people want to do.

Why do you do it?

People pay me to do it. But it's more than that. When I first started as a beekeeper, I had twelve to twenty hives, and I did a rescue from a church. That next winter was a hard one, and every one of my hives died . . . except the rescued hive. Sometimes rescued hives are hardier bees. I'm glad when I get to take them home. I want them in my bee yard. The bees themselves (and the secrets they keep about long-term honeybee survival) are more important than the money.

You don't get stung much, even though you don't wear protective gear. Why is that?

When I arrive to rescue a hive, homeowners ask me things like, "Should we leave the country while you do this?" I tell them, "You don't even have to leave the room!" I'm gentle with the bees. I move slowly. I breathe through my nose, not my mouth. If you don't hurt them, the bees won't hurt you.

What would you like people to understand about your work?

It's an adventure. You *are* going to get stung. Sooner or later, it happens. But if you learn to read their behaviors, you can work with bees without protection. Don't be afraid of honeybees! We need them.

In some parts of the country, rescuing honeybees is not advised. Why is that?

In some places, mostly those with very warm winters, honeybees who've built homes where they aren't welcome have to be destroyed. That's because there's no way to know for sure if those honeybees are the kind of gentle honeybees I rescue (*Apis mellifera*) or a closely related warm-weather strain of bees known for extreme defensiveness (*Apis scutellata*).

Could Mr. Connery's colony have survived the winter in that garage?

Maybe. There was some protection in there, even though the structure had no windows or doors. It's hard to say, because they would have been pretty exposed. They had a better chance back in a hive box.

When you moved the garage-bee comb into a hive box, you carefully arranged it so that the sheets hung in the same order they'd hung on the ceiling. Why?

It's important to maintain the arrangement of the original nest as much as possible. Honeybees keep their young bees, or brood, in the center of the hive. It's easier for them to keep the brood warm there because they can cluster around it. By arranging the bee's new home in the exact order they'd arranged it themselves in the wild, I make it easier for the bees and their brood to survive the move.

What should people do if they find a honeybee hive in their own garage or somewhere else they don't want honeybees living?

Get on the internet and find a local beekeeping association. They can connect you with someone who can safely remove the honeybees alive.

Bee Rescue Resources

Visit the American Beekeeping Federation bee-removal page for information about who to call in most states: https://www.abfnet.org/page/swarms.

Glossary

cells: Hexagonal (six-sided) cups of wax made by honeybees. Sheets of these cells are called comb.

colony: A family of honeybees living together in a hive.

colony collapse disorder (CCD): A name coined to describe a specific set of symptoms observed in failing honeybee colonies. The precise cause of CCD is still unknown.

comb: Wax sheets that form the foundation of a hive. The comb is composed of hexagon-shaped cells that honeybees make for holding pollen, nectar, and honey (honeycomb) or young bees (brood comb). Bees attach comb to a ceiling, wall, or other structure by its sticky wax, and over time further secure it with propolis, a resin collected from plants.

frames: Rectangular supports placed inside managed beehives. Bees build their two-sided sheets of comb in these frames.

hive: A protected space where honeybees live.

hive box: A wooden box in which beekeepers raise honeybees. Each box can hold eight or ten wooden frames and can be stacked to increase space.

honey: A sugary liquid made from flower nectar. Bees use honey as a food source, and beekeepers collect it to eat and sell.

nectar: A sugary substance produced by most flowers and collected by honeybees in order to make honey.

pollen: The male reproductive material of plants.

pollinate: To initiate seed production in flowering plants by transferring pollen grains.

pollinator: Any creature that supports seed production by moving pollen.

queen bee: The only fully developed female bee in a honeybee hive.

swarm: A group of honeybees that leaves an overcrowded hive. Swarms are most noticeable when bees cluster together in a hanging ball, maintaining the shape for the hours or days it takes to find a new home.

wax: a water-resistant substance produced in an organ inside a honeybee's abdomen and used to make comb. Wax is pale yellow when fresh and darkens to brown with age and use.

Author's Note

A few years ago, my husband and I had our house painted. When the painter saw our beehives, he excitedly told us a story. That very day he had started painting another house, and his team had discovered honeybees living in the roof. "Like, thousands of them," he told us.

"What're they going to do?" I asked, worried that his other clients planned to exterminate the bees.

"That's the best part," he told me, shaking his head. "They found some beekeeper guy willing to come and take them out."

I knew immediately that I was going to have to meet that beekeeper. The housepainter put me in touch with the other homeowners, and they put me in touch with the beekeeper, and two days later, I watched Jon Nelson rescue a hive of honeybees. On that day, he used a bucket truck to lift himself, his beekeeping tools, his carpentry tools, and his bee-vac to the top of a two-story home. He ripped apart the roof and removed the bees over the course of one very long and very hot summer day. I was transfixed.

I've since had the pleasure of watching Jon rescue bees, work with them in his backyard apiary, and describe his work in a variety of settings. (Including the home of beekeeper John Connery, pictured to the left.) I learn something new every single time. I'm thrilled to share one of his bee rescues with readers in this book. I hope it inspires you to think about honeybees and their behaviors in new ways.

Sources

A note from Loree: I've been studying, reading about, and keeping honeybees for ten years, and in that time have had the good luck of learning from beekeepers and honeybee researchers alike. Some of what these folks taught me has found its way into this book. To tell the story of this specific honeybee rescue, Ellen and I relied on firsthand observations, photographs, and field notes from several bee-rescue adventures with Jon Nelson, as well as interviews with Jon, his occasional rescue partner Roger Robitaille, and the many homeowners who invited them over to rescue errant bees. We also consulted a lot of books about honeybee biology, hive building, and rescuing. These are the most relevant ones:

Bee, Cindy, and Bill Owens. *Honey Bee Removal: A Step-by-Step Guide.* Medina, OH: Root Publishing, 2014.

Caron, Dewey M. *Honey Bee Biology and Beekeeping.* Cheshire, CT: Wicwas Press, 1999.

Seeley, Thomas D. *Honeybee Democracy.* Princeton, NJ: Princeton University Press, 2010.

Further Reading

Barton, Bethany. *Give Bees a Chance*. New York: Viking, 2017.

Burns, Loree Griffin, and Ellen Harasimowicz. *The Hive Detectives: Chronicle of a Honey Bee Catastrophe*. Boston: Houghton Mifflin, 2010.

Fleming, Candace, and Eric Rohmann. *Honeybee: The Busy Life of* Apis Mellifera. New York: Neal Porter Books / Holiday House, 2020.

Markle, Sandra. *The Case of the Vanishing Honeybees: A Scientific Mystery*. Minneapolis: Millbrook, 2014.

Rotner, Shelley, and Anne Woodhull. *The Buzz on Bees: Why Are They Disappearing?* New York: Holiday House, 2010.

Acknowledgments

A thank-you to Scott Herbert and Chad Whitcomb of Charlton Bee Company, who invited Ellen to photograph a honeybee hive inside a tree, and to Pam Lawson and Larry Doe of Doe Orchards, who called Ellen when bees swarmed on their farm. A special thank-you to Gus Skamarycz for his depth of honeybee knowledge and for the only intentional bee sting Ellen ever received in her quests for photographs.

Thanks also to the entire McVie family for their honeybee hospitality, to John Connery for inviting us to record the rescue of his garage bees, and to Mary Duane, beekeeper extraordinaire, for reviewing this book.

Thank you to Christine Raine for the use of three of her photographs, two of Jon Nelson working in a bucket truck and one of Jon Nelson's full vacuum next to a bee smoker.

For Eilidh and Millie, who waited a long time for this book—L. G. B.

For my babygrands—E. H.

Published by Charlesbridge
9 Galen Street
Watertown, MA 02472
(617) 926-0329
www.charlesbridge.com

Printed in China
(hc) 10 9 8 7 6 5 4 3 2 1

Display type set in Chaloops Chank Diesel
Text type set in Bertold Baskerville by Hermann
    Berthold and Polaroid Markers by Jon Simeon
Color separations and printing by 1010 Printing
    International Limited in Huizhou,
    Guangdong, China
Production supervision by Mira Kennedy
Designed by Jon Simeon

Library of Congress Cataloging-in-Publication Data
Names: Burns, Loree Griffin, author. | Harasimowicz, Ellen, other.
Title: Honeybee rescue: a backyard drama / Loree Griffin Burns;
    photographs by Ellen Harasimowicz.
Description: Watertown, MA: Charlesbridge, [2022] | Includes
    bibliographical references. | Audience: Ages 5–8 | Audience:
    Grades K–1 | Summary: "Honeybee rescuer Mr. Nelson
    relocates a colony of 35,000 bees from Mr. Connery's barn
    back to a hive."—Provided by publisher.
Identifiers: LCCN 2021013809 (print) | LCCN 2021013810 (ebook) |
    ISBN 9781623542399 (hardcover) | ISBN 9781632896100 (ebook)
Subjects: LCSH: Bee culture—Juvenile literature. | Beekeepers—
    Juvenile literature. | Honeybee—Juvenile literature.
Classification: LCC SF523.5 .B87 2022 (print) | LCC SF523.5
    (ebook) | DDC 638/.1—dc23
LC record available at https://lccn.loc.gov/2021013809
LC ebook record available at https://lccn.loc.gov/2021013810